Thank You

In Retrospect

Elif Zor

BookLeaf Publishing
India | USA | UK

Presentation by *BookLeaf Publishing*

Web: www.bookleafpub.com

E-mail: info@bookleafpub.com

ISBN: 9789358739305

First edition 2021

ACKNOWLEDGEMENT

They say, "Hurt people hurt."
I chose not to hurt anyone. Instead,
I wrote poems to let all parts of me that were
hurt
by the boys
that I invited into my heart.
I thought maybe this boy was the one, that man
was the love of my life.
He was to love me one day.
In the end, they all proved me wrong.
For this reason, I thank all the boys that I knew
once upon a time.
I thank my publisher for giving me a chance to
let go of my heartaches.
Throughout the writing process,
I have realized to whom I should have been
thankful for all this time
- that is myself for having the biggest heart in
every single relationship that I was rushed to be
in, by boys I did not understand at all.

Cheers to starting a new chapter

on a clean slate!

E.Z

This book is dedicated to
all who will one day
come to see their
own worth that's eternal
before praising
someone else's
for the sake of restricted love.

**Perfect for singles who are constantly dating to find "the one".*

Dating Drama

When love is what I am,

I see the lights bright; they shine.

When the time is right,

I let love pick me up,

fly me over the moon.

Striving for a cup of coffee now.

From that I get tired, tired of acting happy.
Most mornings, it is the same story:
Different faces, with not a single one
ever happy to see me.

Once the curfew dawns upon me,
In every morning sun all that I see
is the same me, looking for love
despite knowing it is not good for me.
Fun nights lead me
to the most upsetting memories.
My future becomes the now that I walk on
barefoot and scared to feel strong,

Walking over iced cold broken pieces of the
same heart shaped glass that jumped out of
my broken mirror,

instead of self-love.

One by one, piece by piece, in tiny possible
existence of the heartbeats,

I don't see myself singing happy songs
anymore.

Can I hear myself at all?

Who is to say that I don't want to be alone?

Day goes by fast, the night is what I own.

Tonight is going to be another one to leave
together, to avoid being alone.

The heartbeats of us will make the walls
shatter while the strong desires

–Absolutely all the humanely hidden but
real desires mixing with silent tears–

Make their way to hide behind the most
beautiful glowing masks of two very good
looking

fake strangers.

When will the nights come to sweep me off

My feet and where will we go to celebrate
the life that we breathe?

Under the same moon, how many lovers
will sing to wake up the next morning

Only to realize what a failure their night
had been.

To end it all, this morning

I wake up to my own call.

Put a little happy song on to sing along

As I decide to watch the sun rise

all alone.

I bake something so that the scent of it

at least that smell can stick around

with hope in my little heart

that one day I could sing with the man

in the same kitchen

But a man who could hear my heart's song,

dance with me forever and on.

Screaming in Silence

In a world full of fools

Making a judgement

Hovering over same unreal faults

Relentless nights

Connecting the dots

Must be found

Nowhere near common sense

But a big egoistic sea of dead fish

Died from fake trees and human plastics.

Sad faces

Complainers

Wide-mouths

Empty house

In order to connect

Lying gets confused with being truly direct.

What is right cannot be separated

from what is wrong.

Ethics play no role

Everyone has become either a model

or a toy boy.

Can't be seen as a cowboy

Nothing cool stands long

For it is made to be destroyed.

Seeing the bright side in this day and age

is seeing nothing at all.

No breath to take in,

No one bothers to even break in

into their souls,

and their personal cores.

Nothing deep can get above.

Most importantly their own

self made egoist zone.

Walk!

Someone walks faster.

Talk!

You lose a job, you are a loser.

Run!

They make a better runner.

Swim!

Someone watches you over.

Tight jeans,

bikini lines,

When did we forget to feel truly alive?

Get quiet, get some rest.

Tomorrow will be a brand new day

bringing more things unaddressed.

Complaint!

Your life is a mess.

Don't!

You look funny in that dress.

Stress!

More stress!

All life has become

Is a daily dose of things

you need to repress.

Repress,

Forget,

Plug to charge,

Unplug to sleep.

Watch and learn

to become a foreigner to your own throne.

Go out!

Be ready!

Your time is almost up

better prepare to look pretty.

If you are a guy,

Quit being shy.

Get out there, show us all

Your prettiest smile.

Faces up

Down right

Keep up with this world

by bringing your own arrow and bow.

Sinking while singing,

matching while eating,

dating when sobbing.

When did we start to believe really?

Everything is going to be

just alright.

Right.

My Never Lover

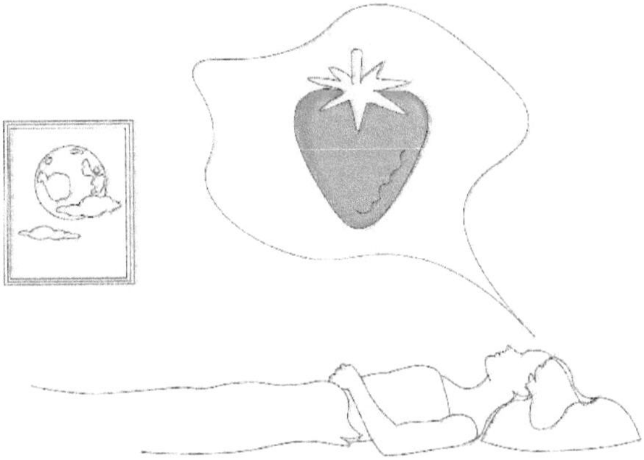

Where there is will, there will be

you.

While you wait for me, I will be

here waiting for you to find me

exist in you.

Things in the nature grow

Growth reminds me of you

Strangled together like the leaves on a tree,

Yet very far apart.

You and I,

We came to this earth to be free.

You are waiting for me as I am aiming for you

I know you are dreaming about me, too.

Momentary thoughts of you will bring me closer

to you.

As you make your way to me,

I will dig mine towards you.

Since we haven't met yet

you haven't known me as I have never seen

you.

Not watching the same sky together

We are here to hope in the dark for awhile.

The moon lights up those same nights

for the lovers

who are lucky to love each other

in their strawberry scented hearts.

We are different, you and I

are probably not ever going to sail together

far.

You live your life as I live mine

We smell the strawberries

Rising from others' hearts

through the same moon light that set us
apart.

My sunset might be your moonlight, or

maybe we are neighbors now.

Who is to say that my hopeless malodorous
heart

will ever smell yours on a fine breezy
night?

This is to you my never lover,

Thank you for making me hopeful

in this never to be relationship of ours.

This never to achieve dream world with you

At least

we are free.

If we were in a relationship, there would be
reasons

to hate you and our hearts would cry

because the life we have lived left us

with a little bag of emotion to survive.

Instead of making me suffer, you chose to

leave me under the cover, alone as it can be.

Hopeless as a romantic gets that

I feel and see

Yet, where there is no relationship , there is
no reason to worry.

For that I am thankful to you for not ever meeting me,

For I realize our love will always continue,

eternally.

I can't wait to smell like strawberry,

not to any

but to my love

who will never meet me.

Forever

Forever closed the door

Behind him after all wasted years.

As he walked away from me now,

His wait did not take long

For he has many forever lovers knocking at his own door.

New forevers for him stopped bothering me

All at once and for all.

Once he decided to walk away

From our dream future

Where all promises burned, ignoring what was burning inside,

Deep inside my own soul.

I

Stood behind the closed door, watching,

He was now fading into darkness,

Leaving all the light for me to grow.

Only then, I could glow.

A new forever knocked at my door.

Randomly, but expected

For the sake of a new love story.

He waited patiently, or should I have said passionately?

Remembering the pain and suffering from before

Hanging at the same door

That brings butterflies to my core.

I try to hide it all.

I asked, "Who is it?"

He answered, "Your forever lover."

I hesitated

When he insisted.

I stopped responding.

He tore down the door to "my forever" now.

After long and endless kisses,

brunches and bunch of happy memories,

getaways and get togethers,

parties and restless love making sessions,

my new forever took the hand of my current presents.

My present to him was the hanging past memories of old lovers creeping at my door.

At first he hesitated, then he insisted, but he did not stop responding to me with his forever lovely symphony.

Years passed by.

Once being my forever got me yet again,

Mixed with another.

I left him with his new lover,

thinking he might have been

someone else's true and passionate

forever lover.

I knew he wasn't mine for the better.

Giving up had never been this easy on me

Maybe it was my heart getting into pieces,

letting go,

not having any high hopes

for the love of my so long lover

being the thoughtless of all

leaving me with my shadows hanging on
the wall.

I ran away behind the closed doors,

faced shadows on the wall.

I tried to run to another lover,

Yet decided not to do so again, never.

Door is shut, walls are built, keys were
broken but now it has made me stronger
than ever.

My new door is there,

there to be mine forever.

Protector, perhaps the forever new lover.

My new forever ended up being the door

I built over all those hopeless lovers.

Counting the days to more of self

self realizations.

Self realizes everything.

Shhh…

My new forever now is at the door,

waving a goodbye to my self-built door,

leaving me with my own self- built door.

Pain that comes from love

does not scare me anymore.

Letting go is the easiest, I decided.

Standing at the door helplessly waiting for
a new forever lasting memory.

Holding on is the hardest, no one wants to
hold on.

Thank God my past relationships

have been so long gone.

Even though I am not scared to have
another one,

I throw my own keys to the bottom of the
ocean for my heart only should belong to
one,

not one hopeless another forever

but it has to be me, myself and I.

Keeping my own heart safe

from all the cheaters, liars

and forever never loving,

Fake

and never real

Always a taker

never trying to be a giver

All the loveless men

alive to fight for their own selfish battles.

I will stand tall against it all

forever strong on my self- built wall.

I Just Read A Poem

I just read a poem

to which my own veil was lifted

in which I held myself for a year

waiting for something to finally appear.

A poem

I just read

offered me a hand to an upward wave.

I came up with the wave until...

It pushed me down again.

Brought me back to earth

in small rain drops.

I am dancing in the rain.

Meanwhile, I forgot how to swim.

My mind was against this dream

Finally,

I left myself all the way in.

Inner courage holds onto my own skin.

This poem I read

mentioned hardships in love.

It is love that was hidden from a woman
who died from a war

with another woman in love

sharing as much emotions for the same man

as the woman who died

torn apart, loving a man

who did not love her back at all

at any cost

he has never mentioned why.

The same love could have cured her

but the woman died, her loneliness being
the only thing left to soar.

I choose to hide

as soon as I come across a dead woman's
words in her heart's devastating tides

of emotions bringing her not the man she
loved,

only suffering that filled her lonely nights

with overwhelming tear drops.

A poem revealed to me

hiding from my own fear and misery

doesn't bring happiness,

but a death to a man

who never dared to love me.

He wanted another woman

leaving me feel like the other.

Hence, there I was leaving him behind,

killing him in my heart

swimming against the waves

trying to get my head above the water.

There I was leaving the man behind

who never dared to give me his past,

neither did he want to laugh with me

together.

I swam with the fish,

swam in the darkest ocean deeps.

Stopping momentarily to breathe

always managing to dive

back inside the oceans of his memories.

Always welcoming me

with all that was going on underneath.

I swam in the ocean until seagulls took me
out because I suddenly lost my breath

blame all this nonsense hopeless but
hopefulness running in my veins.

The seagulls gave me my next reason

to breathe.

They said I was free now

the man I loved finally leaving me,

be me.

I listened as they kept telling me

that I was strong now,

that I knew the infinite possibilities

above and beyond the skies,

"Above and beyond the seas," a fish said

jumping out of the water to make me
believe.

I was then taken by the lions who gave me
lessons on how to hold on to life when
instead I decided to give in.

They filled me with fearless thoughts and
endless boldness that my old self refused to
belong.

"A man has done this to me,"

I blamed the man.

As the lions got their pride together

To bring me to some wolf packs

thinking maybe, they would make

realize it was not the man but

it was me who loved him more

more than I could ever love me.

There I stood in, almost lost myself again

but the wise wolf told me I had given what I
had given and what was there to feel the
pain so deeply.

I stood there watching him move closer.

When he called his pack

to bring me some heart medicine.

"This medicine is good for your heart,"

they said, looking at me.

I looked away.

"This is to protect your heart from all

that an ugly man can rip apart."

I nodded.

Next thing,

I opened my eyes seeing all the strings

the strings were attached

but they were also not very tight.

I walked days and nights to find out

what caused me to see this fight.

Between all of my kind to understand

the reasons that love might have caused.

No answers at hand, cold on my skin,

the burning sun on my face;

I'm barefoot and thin.

I remembered why

I was scared in the beginning.

It wasn't the man who left me,

couldn't be the dead woman's poem

that reminded me,

but the thought of loneliness,

loneliness that I could find myself in

one day could have been the same place

where I found myself today.

Along with all

that the animals have given me,

I remembered

swimming with sharks,

flying with birds,

running with lions,

howling with the wolves.

I liked my loneliness even more than

I could have ever thought of.

They were always in me

where no loneliness could enter freely.

I thanked the poem,

the animals and my loneliness;

Looked at my watch, realizing I had some more time

For more loneliness, I could not get enough.

How could I have known life was getting ready to offer me

the man I am now soon to marry?

Existential Life Crisis

Days Go By

Days go by in this world on this very day

As I look back on my life,

why do I only pray?

I somehow choose to see the failures,
which then leads me
to lose my current energy.
Eventually all my life down the drain
I am now old.
Oh this feeling...
Feeling of being nothing in this world
that I just try relentlessly to explain
fail each time
maybe deep down
I believe I am not nothing at all
afterall.

Feeling like a failure for

that I took the roads

no one traveled alone

any season,

thinking

maybe

I could be a Superstar

who traveled the less traveled roads

all alone

looking like a cool and brave person

that I am

a person who is still alive,

a special kind.

Instead,

I ended up facing my own demon in the eyes,

walked miles over the mountaintops

to fall each time

realizing

I was only made to be broken

fall from the highest highs

so that my feet could touch the ground.

As they said,

I took the less traveled road.

I believe I did only to face the fact

they were all delirious and fraudulent

masters of nothing and no one.

I am all exposed now

facing a world that tells me

I am nobody

with

no talents,

not even one single skill to get close by

to any deity.

Instead,

I am a simple human being

feeling all there is to worry me.

Love, work, men and women

feelings, emotions, wars all over

peaceful looking intimidated pricks

lies and false truths,

too many elephants in our rooms

nothing can be hidden forever

no one is living their best life

for there exists none whatsoever.

Money

Money chose not to come to me.

I decided to listen to the gurus.

Have I been reading a lot of self-help books!

Eventually, I got aggressive to get money.

I put out all the talents possessed by me

hidden from the sights of all that

of my enemy.

Showed the world what it could be

by working in teams,

cleaning houses with my own fingertips,

collecting tips,

smiling at customers

who cared only what to eat,

having drama behind my back

because I loved creating new things;

make a place for everyone to be freely

make someone smile hoping

they smile back at me,

help a kid to learn

so he would learn how to be

a part of this ruthless society.

The times one works

to earn one's own bread and money

is the hardest challenge that I faced

internally.

Losing my jobs because of complainers

and people who gave me no chance

to make myself happy

with all that money I earned

I only became everyone else's desires

forgetting who I was to be.

Had I been different, I would have gone

through the same miserable meaningless

vampire jobs that attentively sucked my

juicy and sweet blood,

non stop.

Shame on me I worked so hard

at doing my job right!

My aim has started off so high

I was going to graduate college

and be a woman who is wise.

I was going to show the world all the skills
and talents that I had possessed

to shock the world to its very core memory.

Thousands of interviews for jobs.

Believing the self could make us weak.

Self love might be true,

but it is the hardest

when everyone around

decides to be freaks.

“Everybody wants to rule the world.”

What a great combination of song lyrics!

In a world full of so called rockstars,

the unwanted hatred for the self

travels through one’s spine,

whirling and twirling around

in electric shock giving a type of spiral.

Colorful but in the dark

trying to shine bright.

Heartless dictators

Lost passions

Silly fairy tales

Hopeless dreams

Epic future planning

Anxiety and with no real meaning

Never spoken failure stories.

Life is all about this and that,

A meaningless self riot

against those who are out of the matrix.

We are against ourselves,

I am.

We are against the other,

I wish.

We want the worse for him and her,

for their gender, type of skin color.

We are hopeless,

I am.

We are not to survive.

I don't think I will.

All the dreams that we had dreamed once

to achieve the highest point in our

stupid lives

I can't even remember what it was.

Now

Silently and steadily

Back to work, deliberately.

Make money

Feed yourself, but first your family

If,

of course

you somehow managed

not ending up broke.

Life is short and sweet,

I wish that was my point.

Sadly, it is not.

This life is here to teach us

along with everybody,

how to suffer in a human body

that is made of tears and painful memories.

What a painful remedy!

It is time you push your limits to the sky;

Otherwise, you might end up dying alive.

These are the best times you keep

That upper lip of yours

stiff,

so they know you are faking to be alive.

Get on your feet!

Work an extra hour to shine bright

In the darkness

Of your own life in dreams.

I read a poem today

a death of a woman because of her love

shed a light on all the pain

I kept inside

so dark but now it is out

in the light.

Hungry Employee

There are no eggs in the fridge

Worse, there is no time.

Time is not something you can buy

While in it you constantly work

to achieve high.

No milk, no eggs, not even sunshine.

In that sense, that kind of productivity does not bring eggs to your fridge.

You do.

Time does not walk into a grocery store to get you eggs,

then place them in your fridge.

You do.

Unfortunately, there is no time to go

buy eggs.

Since eggs can't walk into your fridge,

and time does not deliver,

you are someone with no eggs.

Rather you work to feel like you have
gained.

That same morning brings more time

To make more time

To work more

To hope one day you will have the time

To have a fridge full of eggs

To eat.

Avoiding not to feel like hungry employees

The meaning of the ultimate person

who succeeded.

In the most righteous way,

the most presumed

even if you'd like,

the eggs you are craving

are not to be found there

in your fridge.

Your fridge cries out loud

Tears echo in its empty soulless fridge door

The door has a beer or two to give you

the buzz

To work more

To make time

To get eggs,

True meaning of real success.

Instead of walking to a bodega,

no deli, you choose nowhere to be

You work your life away, baby

With no eggs in

your little overworked skinny belly.

Happy Mornings

are no nests.

Don't you realize eggs don't bring you happiness?

You fail to realize

what you do in this life

is a process to get dressed,

step outside to witness

happiness

that makes

its way to your belly

in the shape of eggs and dairy.

Rest in peace now

You worked all your life to die today.

I wish I could have saved you from

your work,

I could have done that

if you only opened your windows.

I could shine on you daily.

This life brought you no happiness.

It's time you beat your own enemy,

that is you and you consistently.

Why not today

you wake up to the smell,

the very smell of a half burned

toasted bread,

With eggs on the side after you drink

your naturally scented coffee,

cheese and salad that got dressed

for you so you can eat?

You are now finally feeling

the magnificent vibes

of true morning prides without the sounds

your belly not screaming for the end of this

very hopeless employee.

Sprinkle flowers over your table

Feel your senses coming toward your true
prayer

It is in your human nature

Let all the sunshine shining on your face

be a reminder

of the cravings you leave behind,

making your new way towards

this natural blessing and stars

once and for all.

All the hungry workers who work to
achieve success in their breakfast table

instead of a meeting call.

Love Me

Your love is my Pandora,

My cosmic reflection

is that of your aura.

It is my infinite protection.

Infect me with your love

Cut through my deepest fears

My body is yours now

Destroy my battleships

In the shores of nowhere seas.

Take my own sky

Wish upon a star.

Make me blind with your love

No matter what kind of fears

are showing up at your sight.

Come closer

Looking deep in my eyes

See my soul

Know my love for you

Hand in hand with your own heart

The purest heart!

No matter what comes apart,

Goes down

Holds us in vain

Hopeless as my next life

I will still

and always stand by.

All that is mine now

is also what belongs to you.

Fearing from your love

is what I won't ever do.

Your love is my Pandora,

I made you a promise to say it over

and over.

Do I ever forget it,

remind me to love you more than ever.

Let me dissolve in your aura.

My Pandora

The happiest laughter

Sunny days

A baby in need of a mother

Kid like a flower.

Music to my soul

Beat of my heart

Song to the prettiest lyrics

Tempo!

Half note!

Harmony!

The sweetest ever made melody alive!

My sometimes-teenage lover

Only acting like an adult

Whose skin can make me a sinner.

Loving you is all I want to do

In this world and eternally

full of winners and losers

fighters and cowards

here and there

ups and downs

remember not to forget

I will always stand

Stand by you.

You are the only thing

that has the power

to make me blue.

Stars are not enough to show you my love.

Break down the skies

Bring down all the galaxies

Must never question the love in my heart,

for you are the only one.

My Pandora

Skies with sweetest drama.

Ask,

I will do.

Wish,

You will see it, too.

Fear,

I will do everything

to make it disappear.

Cry,

I will be your childhood lullaby.

Laugh,

every moment of it will be in my brain,

Like a photograph.

Love

Love

Love

Me.

Don't promise me your forevers

But for now, tell me

how much you love me.

I have a meaning

because you love me.

Please, love me

When you don't feel like it,

Don't worry.

Show me.

Call me.

Say it to me.

Look at me.

I need it more than ever.

Say you love me.

As you always say, "You and I are free."

Just as I am free to adore you,

you are free to leave me in this cloud

that gets dark and rainy

wet and eerie

without you around me.

My sweet Pandora,

Reaching my hands to you forever

and beyond all forevers together.

Nothing should worry you

for I will always stand by you.

Listening to your sweetest opera,

Your voice,

your sound,

laughter and anger,

speech and your stutter.

I promise

YOU give me the highest fever.

Perfect lover,

Adventurous

always a fantasy seeker,

my own known sinner.

Strongest samurai,

best fighter,

loveliest knight,

owner of all the songs

I sing in the shower.

Brightest mornings

Happiest feelings

All the forgotten lovely lyrics

Unforgettable memories

Futures and dreams

Best films

and romance movies.

All things

beyond our dreams.

Along with all their meanings

You are my Pandora

having nothing inside,

No passion

No love

I wonder...

If you will ever

keep only the very thing

that I will strive

forever.

Your love for me

is the need of a person like me.

Your glazed eyes are making me dizzy

each time you look at me

empty with no sympathy.

You will perhaps love me

one day, call me

to say you are in love with me

hopefully.

Or maybe,

I will someday grow in you,

Look at how you grew in me.

Kitty

Watching you

Nap by the window

Feels almost like

As if this place

Where we are

A place in heaven,

Made for you and me

watching the earth below.

A country sight

Or a view from a high mountain top

By any means and everything aside

What words can better explain

The comfort you give in

Is the love that can easily be seen.

No matter if snow falls,

Winds break our windows

Knock, knock, knock!

How many raindrops had fallen down

Breaking the winds apart?

Door is shaking,

Sound outside is groundbreaking.

With your beautiful cat eyes

I am a brand new human being.

With every kiss,

safe sleeps,

beautiful dreams,

little paws,

soft like softest pillows,

fancier with each meow

making the whole household

living in a happiness cloud.

Thankful for your pink brows,

Distinguished whiskers,

Moustache already full grown.

Thank you for being part of me

my short lived life story.

Your paw paws paint

the most colorfully

fun and exciting

Unforgettable and playful memory.

In my head I want to tell you

outside you see me

playing with you,

my one and only fluffy kitty.

My life is better with you

bringing the heavens to me

You are so pretty

Attentive to my feelings,

make it easy to be a best friend

to a girl like me.

Can’t get over this softest tummy.

Kiss and more kisses on your head

That looks like a mosaic cake

Feeling like the softest snow flake.

Hand In Hand

Hand in hand,

We used to walk the streets

Forever long

Loudly without fear,

silent words.

Love of two happy love birds,

Endless continuing laughter.

Hand in hand, we used to walk

Walk in the streets

Sometimes we would get lost.

Nothing back then

Nothing had a meaning

Just you and I

burning in the hottest flames.

Hot as in love

Smelling the food of the neighborhood

around.

With time,

Change has moved to those streets.

Only echoes of our laughter

took place in the piercing silence.

No laughter like ours has been heard again.

Neighbors never got lost,

Lovers loved in the cold.

Instead of the smell of beautiful food,

Food got burned to ashes,

Food in the neighborhood's oven

since you left my hand

for the longest time being

I kept looking for yours

in the same streets.

At last I realized,

nowhere near these streets

Will I ever see you again,

For the new life you live

that is not with me in it.

To me,

It is all foreign.

As I walk alone now

yet hand in hand

with my brand new friend

a stranger...

I can't help but think about you

a stranger can never replace you.

Last Farewell

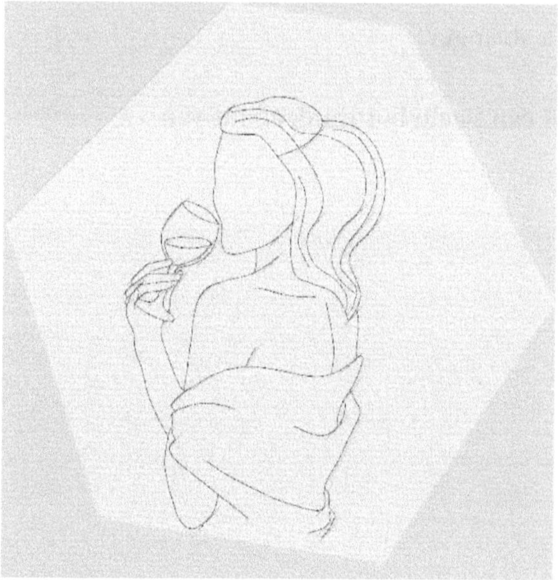

Far away

Close in my face

Look away

Looking through me

Face to face

Do you enjoy it?

Don't hurt me!

Leaves anyway...

Come back

No return guaranteed

Move on

Possibly never again

Left anyway

When nothing went right

Far away

Nothing being said

Made up the feelings

That I pray they fade away.

Move on

I should move on

Leave your phone

It will be fine.

Meanwhile

The sun

The moon

Your lucky star

Galaxies exist

here and beyond

Won't go bright

Without you spinning around

me.

You are a liar

All lies you have said

Are now what I deeply desire

to understand,

Never getting it right.

This time again,

I failed, one more time!

Don't come back!

Almost halfway there

Please go away!

You are my deer in the headlights.

Leave me alone!

Ten feet away

Not anywhere near!

Here not to be your next fear

Fire away!

Hitting my heart

No way!

I love you.

Not fair!

Not this time, I won't disappear.

I don't want you!

I won't hurt you.

Heard it all before!

Saying it all again

Please don't!

Won't stop, I won't.

Won't stop,

I won't stop, either!

Not denying what is yours

But this time

I am only claiming what is already mine.

Your past scars on me

are like wine,

Sweet later on

But please stay with me,

sour or sweet,

for a long time.

Every time you come back to have

This heart of mine...

Do what you want.

I am sorry

From now on

It's my way

From a past I shared with you

I have to move on

To a different one?

That is truly mine

To me it's the most divine!

The road might not get easier

But baby, don't stress

For I will be glamorous and fine.

Just like the sun!

I will burn myself at first

In the end you are shining so bright.

Farewell, love.

I am deaf to your lips.

Alone I raise this glass of my wine.

It is my wish

You and I

Hoping to be together again

Not ever, no never

And...

Ever!

Never to be yet again, intertwined.

Wheel of Fortune

Thanks a lot,

Gaining her trust

by losing mine.

Where existed your heart

nothing is left behind.

As it goes,

as you believe,

as you say it like you are in a dream

Lips move, I am glued

in your deep voice

your words elude.

"This world is cruel, I give in."

Thanks to you

my head is spinning.

Empty tranquility

takes over my own skin.

It is you!

People who are just like you,

such thoughtless acts of who

dies for two,

leaving the third behind

the one you thought you loved, so blind

we are now through.

Leaving behind all my colors

I paint all my colors in blue.

Good for her!

Baking a cake

Puts on a show

What an act!

In it you think you direct,

You write

You own

You play

Your one man show

with her is no mistake.

Yet,

You are still alone in the same bed.

Loneliness can't be cured by

no homemade cake that's built on
something fake.

Nothing gets done

by the seconds of smiles

that are freshly baked

served with cold lemonade

homemade by sweet lies.

Life is more than seconds

in which we live.

Time departures

nothing arrives.

Adventures are good for the soul

As long as they make us feel

Someone

Somewhere

Somewhat

Inside or out

Feel better.

We face the hardship

of seconds, in desires

Make up names for love

feeling all the guilt for the others

Seconds pass by,

Minutes run us over.

What's left behind is all that horror.

You regret

being a cheater.

Now it is her show

It is too late.

She directs,

She writes,

She owns,

You play along.

The wheel of fortune

Spins around.

You are sad,

You don't clap.

Nothing gets done

by faking passing minutes

with fake joy.

When you have no time

to be real,

so real,

even when you fake.

She faked.

Eyes open, fully awake.

Your acts of kindness glows through

just by being you,

the real you,

nothing new.

It's the only side of you

At least that's what I knew.

Until one day

you flew.

One day

she will realize this, too.

Music

In music

we shine

Under the

covers

that is our

skies.

Endless spirals of common energies

From our own crowns to make a life

worth it to live it long, so long.

Live it over and over under covers,

having the bed of our own,

our own bed of flowers.

Music plays

deeper truths of the hearts

spiralling up,

comes out on the surface

of each lovely naked eye.

Opening up the skies,

becoming one into the mother

Our shared mother nature.

Nature of all that smells like

the most beautiful flower.

In it we are her children

Feelings spread all together

over there,

little sprinkles over here.

Down under your feet

life smiles at you

those who are with you

at their hearts music is the most honest clue.

Same beats

at the same time.

All we are hearing is what

we share in our hearts.

Daylight or twilight

Deeper strike, locked in one look

Under a fairy tale starlight.

In Circles We Love

Circles

Some circles make us more
curious

Some make it all more
disastrous

Some just exist

Some we cannot find no meaning

Some we do not look for

Some there

Some above our heads

We are always in that circle

standing in the middle...

Looking ahead to the new bright,

hopeful sunrise

to take its place in the night skies.

In the circle

right there in the middle,

we all stand alone against all that

sun shines on our lives

to find our truly missing

human parts

to one day

become one.

The Search

You look

Look for the

love of your

life.

Searching all along

in these eventful, fruity but lonely

years of your life.

Finally and happily

find the one you think is right for you.

Then, comes the next step

that is to marry.

Tying the knot,

making it right

against all the odds

in your mind

your other versions of you

letting you not decide.

Finally but officially

getting married in front of all people,

feeling on you all the eyes teary

as if you died and come back as a zombie

already.

Looking against all the shining

bright lights,

Leaving behind you is staying up

all those lonely nights

never to be spent alone again

now you are happily married to your

love

and have so much to do to feel sane.

You think you deserve to be happy

Most of all,

you think you deserve to have a family,

like everyone else around you acting very
much happily ever after with their

own little ideal family.

Until one day

out of an ordinary,

you find out your partner

did not love you, truthfully.

That's nothing to worry

Maybe, it was never meant to be.

You two were never a true family.

Your "should not haves" and regrets

begin to take their place.

Constantly but slowly,

your mind dwells on the memory

of your dreams about being

a happy family.

At a night that is yours, yet again lonely.

Where once existed your high hopes

along with all that was for an instant

fulfilling dreams

and the happiest memory.

Leave its place to a garbage that's as dirty

as the streets of New York City.

Your job now

is to look for every single remedy.

Heal your heart

Feel less passionate

May your future lover

be less of a person comparing to the ones

who you now left behind.

Just when you think you will end it now

By getting a divorce

or go through yet another break up,

bumpy roads get tough for your partner

who acts faster, in hurry

out of breath to tell you he is sorry.

Time has come to shatter

all that was planned to shine brighter,
together

dies in the hands of another.

Your husband your forever lover

decides to leave you before you make up
your mind to break up a family.

Your partner begs for your pardon to kill it,

the relationship once and for all dies.

He kills when you on the other hand

were trying to build it on your own

from the ground

by having nightmares alone

in your bed thinking

your husband will eventually stop

stop being so monotone.

Yet again, another death in your hands

Relationship you thought

you would water to grow

like a little newborn sparrow

dies in your hands

because of yet another arrow,

shot by another thoughtless man

who chose to live in his own shadow.

All the chances taken

Until chances do not want

to exist anymore.

Change gives us hope,

then leaves us all alone.

However, it does not take long

Because there are plenty of fish in the sea,
all around.

You keep swimming, you just keep
swimming until you realize

you have been smoking

so much smoke...

Just keep smoking

Your own lungs cannot even carry.

How could another person who lives with it
daily?

For a while you get down,

then you get right back up.

Face another Valentine's Day

Never with the same gal.

Finally giving up on love

to be able to choose the best

of what is left

Take her or him to save our lonely life,

Lonely as tiny pieces of dust

living once in a big sanitized heart

now turning into a dust pun.

Freely moving

Yet limited in a full dreaming state,

that is hard to undo.

No daughter, neither a son,

Only with the daily rising sun.

Hang In There

Days gone by

Nothing to look forward

Nothing completely

to hang on to

for no cause.

Not a single action taken;

Final endings hanging on

With endless to-do lists

Unexpected results occurring.

Fish out the sea

for no reason

while you wait for a delivery.

All day a cat tells you

he could make a better salary

if he was not your home buddy.

But a guy who worked hard, daily

Not hesitating, proudly.

Time

One problem

solves another.

Next, however,

is yours forever.

Until someone walks in and says,

"Let's solve this together!"

One plus one is two

as the orange days turn to blue,

Blue turns to the darkest sky

until it is us who dream awake to start

a new beginning.

A new single opening eye

Slightly waking up to the yellow color

Changing colors of the same sky.

Time flies.

Another juncture

Date is not known

Where once fell an orange leaf

is where the leaf now turns to green.

One, only one

one single point at a time.

Drop the clock

Time has now flunked.

Make time to lose no time.

May realize that you are out of time

It has now already gone by

Time after time,

instead of saving it,

Perhaps we are running slowly

burned out more quickly.

Fine, so fine!

Life is a cradle where we find fun.

Fun, oh fun!

Time took it away to turn into a bind.

Bind, baby, bind!

Bind to the life where you have time.

Stop killing your time!

As it is regardless of how much money you have, it's not your lifetime.

Primetime

Shows that take so much of your time

Instead of living, living truly

to what you deserve to live

simply

You are living your one life

with no spare time.

Buy, baby, buy!

Give a little time,

so you could buy

some more time.

Stay awake to make up

all your wasted youthful years

so you can sleep in the future

in some better period of time

somehow.

I Met A Woman

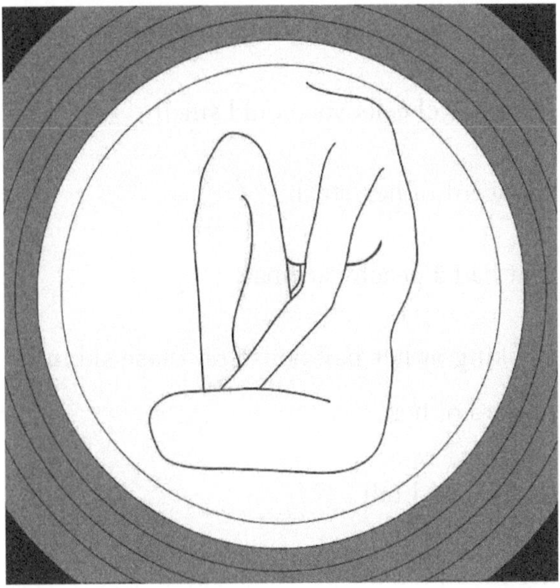

I met a woman today

I met her when she dressed herself up

to hide the pain she felt inside

for the time being.

She put on a mascara to survive

to hold her tears back

tears desperately wanting to come down

from her cheeks you could smell

the scent of her blush

that had a peachy aroma.

Looking at her nail polish on those skinny
fingers of her

easily could tell

her mood for the previous days,

and where it was heading.

To a brand new trauma

bit by bit, every nail had to go

eaten nail polish was never a good sign

to a woman whose beauty hid behind

the scenery it had given to all of her enemy

the other women, maybe.

Her shoes, her goddamn shoes

the most torturing shoes

that collected her pain in all that

her feet bled from all that

scar and bruise.

Just like her once kindred soul

In those shoes

even pain looked sweet

as if she covered it with concrete.

More than that

a hidden secret

of her little feet

in those shoes, they would bleed.

She liked it.

She bared the pain and walked for miles

to be loved in it

as if pain meant her, nothing.

For her man, she felt it

every time she blinked

her pain traveled

to her every single little heartbeat

yet, she would hold on to the pain

never letting it go for that her man loved

her

very,

very deep.

I met another woman today

who wore her heart on her puff sleeves

By the way, she spoke to me

unlike the previous lady,

She told me where

she had last seen her lover

years before she gave up on him.

She was a lone wolf

as she described her relationship with him.

In her words I lost her

when I tried to understand.

She was married with three kids

How did loneliness break into her dreams?

She wore an expensive bag

screaming all she wanted was to brag.

When I asked her about the bag,

she disregarded me to say

it was nothing more than a bag

that she could wear

to fill in the cracks

in her secluded heart.

I could have had the same bag as her

if I wanted it so bad.

As a present, she shared all that was in her empty little but expensive bag.

with her lonely dreams.

She said she wanted to call someone.

Suddenly,

turned to me and said,

"Hopefully, when I get home, my second husband is back."

She wasn't a lonely girl,

but her inner child craved some love

behind all that was seen,

the bag, the puff sleeves, her ignorant insults even .

What she wore on that day

could only cover her skin.

The bag she offered to give me

could not have been any girl's dream.

Expensive yet empty inside

with a borrowed napkin

to deal with the hidden tears coming out

rather than staying in.

Oh, those damned tears

as if they waited to embrace her happiness

unexpectedly, letting out all that of her

obsolete worry.

Coming down the stairs,

I saw a young woman who asked me

for help.

She was young and drunk on love.

She asked me to call her ex

ask him where he had been.

She asked me if I had seen her ex

because she still passionately and

secretly loved him.

I passed her by

not saying anything but a simple sorry

waving goodbye.

Another woman followed,

whom I met in a little cafe called,

Little Sparrow

She told me she had never been wed

due to her sickness in the idea of fate.

She decided to ace her wealth

after losing it to her beloved, her health.

“But now...”, I heard her opening up

to me,

her wealth had left her in need of a man

who meant nothing

but a heartbreak in her own love history.

Her heartbreaks couldn’t possibly cure

all the sickness in her

while all the boys she had come across

could and were able to

leave her without a doubt

to die some day

on her own

while those boys made love to another skin

with no soul,

beautiful candy smell perfumes of other
women

kept taking over those men's feet up from
tiled hotel room floors.

How many was enough

even the men did not know...

No regret

No faults to accept

Credit cards did not buy her memories

memories of love

she could not collect.

"Money is not everything,"

I heard another woman saying,

"I am independent and very giving.

I give to those who are in need and pain

but I got shot by a man

who had never ever given.

Instead, he stole everything

to be even."

"Not a penny

not one full day of his time

all he did was playing

with my stupid heart

that is good enough to be staying

no matter how much pain

we waited for him to love me

realizing that was waiting in vain.

Sometimes, I am even surprised

To find myself praying.

I need God to cure all my pain,

but then why do I still count on this man

who has been driving me insane?

I love him enough

to lose myself in his deadliest and

most venomous men game.

He is my love who comes around me

like mosquitoes during a hurricane."

"What I pray for is a heart

for the ones with none.

No expectation is high.

All I want is a day to remember,

the days when I loved myself better

like a woman that I used to be

before I met a guy who violently

stole me

from me.

I guess all I want is my heart back

Since it is of no use to him.

He thinks I carry my heart

So, he could easily break in."

After meeting all these women,

I closed my apartment door behind me.

Thinking not to think a lot

about all this suffering of my own kind

I could not help, but cried.

They all helped me to find

the woman who resided in me

who felt all that was felt

in the heart-shaped glasses of the women

I've met.

My face, my soul, my heart

sound and vision.

I guess all that should be remembered

is a little girl who was born a fighter

growing up to a world where

she now needs to surrender.

Instead, men

have all that is visible power.

To understand a woman

a woman needs to be loved as a human

as she is one day

going to be someone's mother,

someone's lover.

Someone else's friend, a beautiful teacher,

infinite amount of a giver

and a perfect receiver.

But in the future she will find her star

to shine bright like the moon at a night sky

to prove everyone she is not only here

to suffer greatly.

She is here to become something bigger.

Not a beggar!

Perhaps the perfect

hugger, kisser, dancer, singer

your passionate, trustworthy, one

and only one

true lover.

Social Media

Fancy words

made up worlds

too easy to get left behind.

No stopping, always be alert!

Dignifies, melts,

pods stir

What and for what reasons

do we give in?

Carelessly, fast and purposely

why and who we hurt

is no falsifying

it is only the new age living.

In a world like this,

who is winning?

Everyone flirts

yet no one listens.

Not an extrovert,

neither could succeed at being an introvert.

Your new social media alert!

Sounds, vibrations, clicks and likes

no word is enough to tell the world

who is here to eat an expensive dessert

and who is a living,

wise man dying as an expert.

Senses...

Losing our senses.

In silence we are now connected

to future tenses.

In connection, separately ignorant

no pictures carry a real value of

any kind of dignity.

Picture it

in your mind,

try to live with it

online or not.

Senses...

Come to your senses...

In silence, bring into your attention

that is pure of pretension

with all your good intentions.

Full of fresh air with no friction.

When nothing you hold on to

turns into a post to be liked,

nothing true you receive

but a mental block.

Believe you are not the kind

who live to leave the dark.

Take a slow one step

into your screen light.

Tonight

leave all that social media behind.

Who are you to judge someone else's clock?

Death!

In silence, we hide our death.

Morning glories only are perfect

with pictures that come with

countless hashtags.

Your mood can affect

the millions who will never know your love

for the beautiful sunrises you

in your vision collect.

Sense your likes, hide the fears

Only those who make jokes with their own tears

will survive against those, who make fun of

someone else's intelligence.

Alert, awake, stay up.

Next day, wake up to blend in

for love or hate,

take a left to take it all right in.

Make today count by being right

as if the imaginary world of yours

is eating you up.

Don't feel down.

If you do, bring everyone down with you.

If you are feeling happy,

Tag a friend who would love to hear it, too.

Get inspired, get ahead.

All those haters are generally

all bark and no bite

leaving you feeling all that they don't like

you have all reasons to worry.

Select!

Lose your enemies to select

to hold on to your intellect.

Mind over body, body over your head

feels like a breeze on your hard

earned butter and bread.

Are we really glad to be blessed

or are you blessed to have no self-respect?

Shadow Work Prayer

Future to all

Future that I don't know

Bless my body

Bless my soul

Nothing worse comes from

what I do not allow.

Clean me from others' overshadow.

I accept my sorrows

Accept my own

Walk on a path

with my own pebbles

carrying my own lucky stone.

Realize what I have,

where I belong.

Maybe I am wrong

but I'm sure of it all.

My decisions will land me on a road

where my wrong decisions

can clear horizons,

beyond all that's above.

Not an expert on any gold

The only thing that is shining is me

I am on a hold.

Needing time to find balance

has never been so cold.

Just when there could not be any more challenges,

I think

all I start to see again

is people with their big fake

empowering egoes.

I welcome my own!

Ex lovers, secret desires

past memories, happy sadnesses,

angry faces, nervous breakdowns,

past troubles,

future messed up thought patterns,

healthy decisions

with crucial disappointments.

I greet you all!

Instead of in my home

digging a hole,

I shout at you loudly,

The biggest "Hello!"

Welcome home!

Stay with me for awhile

until the wind stops blowing

until rivers hang on to their own flowing

until mountains stop growing.

Blow the past on my face, blow!

Let me take you out one by one

after realizing

not enough tears will do it

wet tears on my pillow.

Face to face

Eye for an eye

Tooth for a tooth

Let's face this case

by bringing myself to one single point of

the truth.

Let me carefully caress

this memory and that one from my past

all might be meaningless

but…

Why hold on to it when it can kill me

in your prettiest dress?

When is it going to be enough

to start a new life

after ending it all kindly and nice?

Until I am ready for the next test

I am willing and able never to rest.

Take a step back

to see the bigger picture.

Find the missing pieces

of a long lost puzzle.

Certain angles are better

How about facing everything

in an honest manner?

Alone, but together

with myself and my shadow side forever

to work for something better.

Remember...

Remember it all!

Remember your point of start

where you wanted to end up.

Focus closely on where you got stuck.

That way I know when to surrender,

when not to stop

being a true warrior, a firefighter

against the flames that I stepped

over and over.

Letting them burn with my own anger

for the longest time ever

not realizing no fire got me in trouble

It was my doing it to hurt myself in a way
that was so crucial.

No one could hurt me

if I was never surrendered.

A dark corner

now it gets lighter.

Connection is never completed

with an ugly truth sayer sitting with a
naysayer

Both familiar

in the same room, together

looking at me as if I am a stranger.

All I could tell myself was,

“Remember...“

Remember where not to end up

Where you don’t want to go

Who to never trust

To whom you can be like yourself

forever.

Fake or flake

A new chapter starts with my being

so direct

Not with this one

with that person to blame

All that is fake

will have no room

to be fake or

one day to flake.

With all that was no reason to worry

I can sing now and make a birthday cake.

There will be no me

nobody who loves me

no time to take a break,

if I don't face the challenges that made me,

me.

All that is needed is to show the world

once a mistake

never stays a mistake.

I am changing

magnificently!

9 789358 739305

Printed by Libri Plureos GmbH in Hamburg,
Germany